Pebble® Plus

HOW **FOOD** GETS FROM **FARMS** TO **STORE SHELVES**

by Erika L. Shores

Consultant: Nancy Grudens-Schuck, PhD
Associate Professor, Agricultural Education and Studies
Iowa State University, Ames, Iowa

CAPSTONE PRESS
a capstone imprint

Pebble Plus is published by Capstone Press,
1710 Roe Crest Drive, North Mankato, Minnesota 56003
www.mycapstone.com

Library of Congress Cataloging-in-Publication Data
Cataloging-in-publication information is on file with the Library of Congress.
ISBN 978-1-4914-8428-9 (library binding)
ISBN 978-1-4914-8436-4 (paperback)
ISBN 978-1-4914-8440-1 (ebook PDF)

Editorial Credits
Jill Kalz, editor; Juliette Peters and Katelin Plekkenpol, designers;
Morgan Walters, media researcher; Laura Manthe, production specialist

Photo Credits
Capstone Studio: Karon Dubke, 17, Cover; Shutterstock: Alexander Mazurkevich, (bananas) 3, bibiphoto, 9, Fotokon, 6, Henryk Sadura, 16, Jerax, 22-23, Jiri Hera, 15, lzf, 20, MarclSchauer, 8, MO_SES Premium, 18, MSPhotographic, 5, My Portfolio, 13, Orhan Cam, Cover, Orientaly, cover, Paul J Martin, 19, PhIllStudio, 12, photographer, 11, Sailom, 14, smereka, 7, smuay, (leaf) 3, solarseven, back cover, 1, Taina Sohlman, 10, Volt Collection, 21

Note to Parents and Teachers

The Here to There set supports national curriculum standards for science and social studies related to technology and the roles of community workers. This book describes and illustrates the journey our food takes from farms to stores. The images support early readers in understanding the text. The repetition of words and phrases helps early readers in understanding the text. This book also introduces early readers to subject-specific vocabulary words, which are defined in the Glossary section. Early readers may need assistance to read some words and to use the Table of Contents, Glossary, Read More, Internet Sites, Critical Thinking Using the Common Core, and Index sections of the book.

Printed and bound in Canada.
009369FRS16

TABLE OF CONTENTS

Where Food Comes From

What do you like for breakfast?

Milk, cereal, and fruit are

favorite breakfast foods.

How does this food get

from farms to store shelves?

The food we eat is raised
on farms. Farmers plant and grow
crops and fruit. Livestock farmers
raise animals for meat or eggs.

Collecting Milk

Dairy farmers raise cows for milk. The farmers use machines to get the milk from the cows.

milking machine

Milk is collected in tanker trucks. It is processed and packaged into containers. Trucks deliver the containers to stores.

tanker truck

Making Cereal

Farmers harvest crops

when they are ripe.

Trucks take corn, oats, wheat,

and other cereal grains to mills.

The grains are turned into flour.

Food companies buy the flour
to make their products.
Breakfast cereal is made
from cereal grain flour.

bags of flour

14

Cereal is packaged into boxes.
Workers load them onto trucks.
Truck drivers deliver the boxes
to stores.

Traveling Far

Bananas and other fruits may take long trips to stores. They get picked, boxed, and loaded onto ships.

They travel across oceans.

Then trucks bring the fruits to stores.

Working Together

Farmers grow our food.

Truck drivers deliver it to stores.

Workers put it on store shelves.

Many people work together

to get our food from here to there.

GLOSSARY

crop—a plant farmers grow in large amounts, usually for food

dairy—a farm where cows are raised for their milk

grain—the seed of a cereal plant such as wheat, rice, corn, oat, or barley

harvest—to gather crops that are ripe

livestock—animals that are raised for their meat, eggs, or milk

mill—a building that has machines to grind grain into flour or meal

package—to place into plastic containers, cartons, or boxes

process—to put through a series of steps; milk is processed so that it is safe to drink and ready to be sold at stores

READ MORE

Kalman, Bobbie. *Food and Farming Then and Now.* From Olden Days to Modern Ways in Your Community. New York: Crabtree Publishing Company, 2014.

Ready, Dee. *Farmers Help.* Our Community Helpers. North Mankato, Minn.: Capstone Press, 2014.

Taus-Bolstad, Stacy. *From Grass to Milk.* Start to Finish. Minneapolis: Lerner Publications, 2013.

INTERNET SITES

FactHound offers a safe, fun way to find Internet sites related to this book. All of the sites on FactHound have been researched by our staff.

Here's all you do:

Visit *www.facthound.com*

Type in this code: 9781491484289

 Check out projects, games and lots more at **www.capstonekids.com**

CRITICAL THINKING USING THE COMMON CORE

1. What would happen if farmers stopped growing grains? (Integration of Knowledge and Ideas)

2. Describe the trip milk takes to get to a grocery store. (Key Ideas and Details)

INDEX